STRENGTHENING
your
FAITH

STRENGTHENING *your* FAITH

A Toolkit For Believers

TABITHA HENTON LAMB

Strengthening Your Faith
A Toolkit For Believers

Copyright © 2022 Tabitha Henton Lamb.

References: Merriam-Webster Thesaurus and online Thesaurus.com

Bible versions

Since the King James Version is used throughout, the following
acknowledgment prescribed by the publishers in the front
inside cover on the Copyright page may be used:

The scriptures quoted in this book are taken from the King James
Version. The King James Version is in the public domain.

Please note that KJV has no quote marks when someone is speaking

Contents

Introduction

The profundity of the gospel is seen in its simplicity. The message? Let him come who will come, let him who is thirsty drink from the fountain of life.

For God so loved the world, that he gave his only begotten Son, that whosoever believeth in him should not perish, but have everlasting life. For God sent not his Son into the world to condemn the world; but that the world through him might be saved (John 3:16-17).

God the Father demonstrated extravagant love for humanity in sending His Son Jesus. All who accept His love will receive rewards beyond what they can ask or think. The love of God is the artistry of His affection if we would surrender our all to Him. Its beauty is woven into the fine tapestry of life, unlike anything the human heart could even fathom. It will never be exhausted over time or even eternity. It will cause the seeker to trade all of their sorrows and human desires for a taste of such love. All it takes is to simply believe. That will free our heart, and allow it to experience a love so divine, so amazing.

Above all, God desires truth in our inner parts. You may ask what is truth? Jesus provides the answer when He says, *"I am the way, the truth and the life. No one can come to the Father but through Me"* (John 14:6 NKJV). He is the way to salvation, to freedom, joy, peace, love, righteousness, and true fulfillment. He is the giver of healing, wholeness, and restoration. On a true journey with Him, regardless of our past mistakes or mishaps, He has promised to make all things beautiful in their time.

These chapters are designed to light a flame to the candle of our hearts. They remind us we are a branch plucked out of the fire of opposition in this life as we stand for God. They remind us of what He has provided for us. They encourage you not to give up on God or His plan for your life or the redemption of humankind on earth. He is not slack concerning His promises. We are to stand and to remain faithful until the end.

We have a battle plan in place to firm up our stance. It is founded on the Word. It will renew our mind and heart. It will help us pray without ceasing, to wake up each day with one overall mission: to surrender all, to bring down the Glory of God in our lives. This is the prayer of the penitent heart. Not, "Lord, rescue or deliver me or keep me away from dreadful things but, more importantly, secure Your Glory in me that men may see my good works and glorify our Father who is in Heaven."

There is nothing worth giving up on God for. Not loss, illness, hurt, pain or disappointment. There is nothing that can separate us from His love. His Word says, *"Blessed is the man who is not offended in Me"* (Matthew 11:6). Let us be strong in these challenging times, fit for His service and obedient to His will. Let us see our trials and tribulations as a shaping of the character of Christ in us and an opportunity for transformation.

One of the weapons in our spiritual armor is the belt of truth buckled around your waist (Ephesians 6:14). I'd like you to think of it as your tool kit which holds various spiritual tools for service. Will you join me as we sharpen our tools in our tool kit? They will help us acquire a better understanding of His Word and its application to the pressures of life. Thus we arm ourselves for times of suffering. We may come to draw upon the purpose of patience and fasten our eyes upon Christ's endurance as He did the will of His Father. Our spiritual fruit will begin to flourish as we empty out the desires of the human heart and cultivate a heart focused on the heart of our Heavenly Father.

Let us therefore be properly equipped for service in His name, and strengthened in our stance against all the wiles and schemes of the adversary. Come and take this journey with Him empty to discover the vastness of His magnificent love.

The Word and Its Use

In the beginning was the Word, and the Word was with God, and the Word was God. The same was in the beginning with God. All things were made by him; and without him was not any thing made that was made. In him was life; and the life was the light of men (John 1:1-3).

This was the disciple John's introduction to his gospel. The "Word" he speaks of comes from the Greek *logos,* and in this context, it is Jesus Christ. All things came into their existence through Him, and without Him nothing comes into being. The Word is the sole means by which reality has its existence. He is the Creator of all things, and before there was any creation, the Word was.

Jesus Christ is the Messiah, the Son of God and believing in Him we have life in His name (John 20:31). Jesus is the revelation of the word and the eternal creator of all things. He is the object of our faith. He is more than a depiction of God: He is God. Jesus is the subject by which the Word of God is written. If we are truly seeking to know Him, what better way than to find ourselves daily in His Word! Just as the deer pants for the water brooks, seeking to quench its thirst and find protection, so must our souls long desperately after God Psalms 42:1.

Hebrews 4:12 says the Word of God is alive and active.

> *For the word of God is quick, and powerful, and sharper than any twoedged sword, piercing even to the dividing asunder of soul and spirit, and of the joints and marrow, and is a discerner of the thoughts and intents of the heart.*

The word "alive" means "effective, powerful, producing or capable of producing the intended result." The Word of God is alive because God is alive, and we are made alive spiritually and eternally when we are born again. The Word of God is also the Sword of the Spirit (Ephesians 6:17), sharper than a double-edged sword. It is our offensive weapon against the assaults of the enemy. It is the weapon Jesus used when tempted by Satan in the Wilderness. The power of God's word can pierce and penetrate the human soul. It inspects our internal dialogue and our deepest hidden secrets. It also judges the state and attitude of the heart.

The application of His Word brings about His intended purpose. It produces supernatural change within the life of a person. It brings forth abundant living. It has the power to penetrate deep into our internal being to judge our hearts and intents. It sustains man, produces faith, gives him the freedom to accomplish the will of God, brings about spiritual birth, and abides with him. It convinces, converts and comforts. It brings the prideful to humility, and conforms the sinful to obedience. It reveals to us our deepest thoughts and purposes. It is activated in our lives when we receive it. It is more than a history of events. It is the communicative efforts God uses to interact with humanity.

His Word must take deep root into our lives and over our thoughts and actions as we submit to Him, trusting in Him to transform us. His Word is not something we should hear and forget. We must commit to implementing the fulfillment of it.

For if any be a hearer of the word, and not a doer, he is like unto a man beholding his natural face in a glass: For he beholdeth himself, and goeth his way, and straightway forgetteth what manner of man he was. But whoso looketh into the perfect law of liberty, and continueth therein, he being not a forgetful hearer, but a doer of the work, this man shall be blessed in his deed (James 1:23-25).

The Word of God is the greatest rescue plan ever known to man. It is filled with beauty, history, poetry, love stories and knowledge of what is to come. It secures the believer's belt of truth, fortifies the shield of faith, enables the sword of the Spirit, empowers the breastplate of righteousness, equips the helmet of salvation and sanctions the path for our gospel shoes. His Word is a lamp unto our feet and a light unto our path. It makes our pathway prosperous before us. God rewards those who diligently seek after Him. It reveals to us the eternal nature and character of God and His plan and will for humanity. It provides us with the roadmap to eternal life. It shows us the posture of the heart required to please Him. It defies the will of Satan. The Word is the foundation of our faith. We are to fortify our lives with it daily.

Our love for God is really in response to His love for us. We love Him only because He always has and will continue to love us. His love is not to be measured by human terms. It is hard for humans to grasp this kind of love outside of an encounter with Jesus and His precious Holy Spirit; however, it is possible. In this, we understand God's love. When we talk about God's Eternity, we talk about something more significant than just time. For when we say God is infinite, we say that God is self-existent and has no beginning. He derives His existence or His being from no other source; instead, He has the power to be all and all in and of Himself. His love transcends time and space, and there are no boundaries to obstruct it.

> *For I am persuaded, that neither death nor height, nor depth, nor any other creature, shall be able to separate us from the love of God, which is in Christ Jesus our Lord* (Romans 8:38-39).

There is nothing that can separate us from His love, not our corrupt nature, our choices in life, generational curses or slanders from Satan. So we have a choice. We each can come to Him willingly through Jesus with no fear. There are things we can do in life to hurt His heart, but even in that, there is absolutely nothing we can do to cause His love to separate from us. His love is immeasurable:

> *For as high as the heavens are above the earth, so great is His lovingkindness toward those who fear Him. As far as the east is from the west, so far has He removed our transgressions from us Isaiah 55:9.*

God wants us to know Him. To understand a person is to love them truly. Why would He expect us to love Him as His children without taking the time to reveal Himself to us as He so exquisitely has through scripture, through the very image and likeness of His Son Jesus. Jesus said this in response to Philip's request to see the Father:

> *Have I been so long time with you, and yet hast thou not known me, Philip? he that hath seen me hath seen the Father; and how sayest thou then, Show us the Father?* (John 14:9)

Why make the effort to go to such lengths to reveal yourself to someone you do not intend to ever know you, or to learn of your ways and doings? How can you have a relationship with such a one? No, this is not our Father. So Jesus is the revelation of God to us. *"No man hath seen God at any time; the only begotten Son, which is in the bosom of the Father, he hath declared him"* (John 1:18).

When it is released, the word has the dynamic power to accomplish God's purpose.

> *So shall my word be that goeth forth out of my mouth: it shall not return unto me void, but it shall accomplish that which I please, and it shall prosper in the thing whereto I sent it"* (Isaiah 55:11).

So fasten your belt of truth through the following scriptures and meditate on them daily. Wear the word like a garment, and literally become it. *"You will also declare a thing, And it will be established for you; So light will shine on your ways"* (Job 22:28). So declare these words out loud into the atmosphere:

> Greater is He that is in me than he that is in the world 1 John 4:4.

> I can do all things through Christ who strengthens me Philippians 4:13.

> For this reason, was the Son of Man made manifest that He might destroy the works of the Devil 1 John 3:8.

> He that fears is not made perfect in love for perfect love cast out all fear 1 John 4:18.

> God did not give me a spirit of fear but of power of love and of a sound mind 2 Timothy 1:7.

I have the mind of Christ and I hold the thoughts feelings and purposes of His heart 1 Corinthians 2:16.

No weapon formed against me shall prosper and every tongue that rises against me in judgment I will show it to be in the wrong Isaiah 54:17.

Jesus said, "In the *world you will have tribulation; but be of good cheer, I have overcome the world*" (John 16:33). We may as well settle in our minds that we are in a battle between the Divine and the Diabolical. Gird up the loins of your mind and prepare for a fight until the end. Use the Word of God as your weapon of defense and offense against all the onslaughts of the devil. We cannot afford to be ignorant of his devices and neither do we belong on his territory. Rather, we choose to dwell in the secret place of the Most High and abide under the shadow of the Almighty. We can say of the Lord, "He is my God and my refuge; in Him will I trust."

We cannot afford to be weak and lax in our faith. We must fuel ourselves daily to use the word with power and authority at any given moment and make the Word of God part of our internal makeup, our spiritual armor. Commit key scriptures to memory until they are part of your belief system and let them govern your desires, thoughts, feelings, emotions, will, deeds and intents.

We cannot afford to be in the process of getting ready. No, we must always be ready and on guard, vigilant, aware because our enemy goes about as a roaring lion seeking whom he may devour I Peter 1:8. It is a fight until we enter our eternal state. We win in and only through Christ Jesus. We are to be tucked away so tight in Him that the enemy has nothing in us. We are to be completely submerged in the fruit of the Spirit until every open place is sealed in Him.

There are some things that may be delayed in life and some which may never come into fruition; however, we are to be secure in God and His plan for us. We must model ourselves on the founders of our faith who died in faith not having seen the promise but being assured it would be fulfilled – though not in their generation.

We must get to the place that we desire to fulfill the will of the Father more than our human desires, more than the next promotion, house, car or life's finest comforts. Jesus said, *"For what shall it profit a man, if he shall gain the whole world, and lose his own soul?"* (Mark 8:36). May this scripture put life into perspective for us.

Tool #2

Wisdom

Wisdom is an attribute we are told to seek above all things because it is more precious than the rarest of commodities. The book of Proverbs is a great start for finding wisdom.

How much better is it to get wisdom than gold! and to get understanding rather to be chosen than silver! (Proverbs 16:16).

Wisdom is the principal thing; therefore get wisdom: And with all thy getting get understanding (Proverbs 4:7).

Yea, if thou criest after knowledge, and liftest up thy voice for understanding; If thou seekest her as silver, and searchest for her as for hid treasures; Then shalt thou understand the fear of the LORD, and find the knowledge of God. For the LORD giveth wisdom: out of his mouth cometh knowledge and understanding (Proverbs 2:3-6).

Now the wisdom of the world is vastly different from the wisdom of God, "*For the wisdom of this world is foolishness with God. For it is written, He taketh the wise in their own craftiness*" (1 Corinthians 3:19). And again, "*The Lord knoweth the thoughts of the wise, that they are vain*" (1 Corinthians 3:20).

So the kind of wisdom we seek should be Godly wisdom. His wisdom equips us to prepare for our eternity with Him. We are to exchange our earthly values for Godly ones, for after all we are essentially citizens from another Kingdom. Godly wisdom is to see life from God's perspective and clothe ourselves with it. It often requires us to do what is contrary to our natural impulses because its focus is not set on the preservation of self but on the Kingdom of God. We are successful in this once we make a strong commitment to crucify our flesh daily and to be set apart from the world.

The primary way to learn about His wisdom is naturally by consuming it, tasting and eating the Word. Just as the unfolding of His Word brings understanding to the simple (Psalm 119:130), so should we immerse ourselves in it and allow it to permeate our thought life and conversations:

> *Let the word of Christ dwell in you richly in all wisdom; teaching and admonishing one another in psalms and hymns and spiritual songs, singing with grace in your hearts to the Lord* (Colossians 3:16).

Now, while we get our knowledge from various sources, we are to acquire wisdom from God. What's the difference? Knowledge is "information gained through experience, reasoning, or acquaintance, while wisdom as "the ability to discern or judge what is true, right, or lasting." While knowledge is knowing how to accomplish a task, wisdom is knowing when and how to use our knowledge. One can be knowledgeable without being wise but wisdom depends on knowledge for its substance. Wisdom then is the fitting application for knowledge.

> *See then that ye walk circumspectly, not as fools, but as wise, Redeeming the time, because the days are evil. Wherefore be*

*ye not unwise, but understanding what
the will of the Lord is* (Ephesians 5:15-1).

How do we acquire wisdom? The Apostle James tells us to simply ask God for His wisdom in faith believing that He will give it:

*If any of you lack wisdom, let him ask of
God, that giveth to all men liberally, and
upbraideth not; and it shall be given him.
But let him ask in faith, nothing wavering.
For he that wavereth is like a wave of the
sea driven with the wind and tossed. For
let not that man think that he shall receive
any thing of the Lord. A double minded
man is unstable in all his ways* (James
1:5-8).

When you ask in faith and you are single-minded and stable, you are person who is anchored in the righteousness of Christ.

*But of him are ye in Christ Jesus, who
of God is made unto us wisdom, and*

righteousness, and sanctification, and redemption (1 Corinthians 1:30).

However, the reverse happens when you act out of doubt and unbelief; you become unstable and double-minded. But I ask you, what reason do you have to doubt God's integrity and truthfulness when He has proven Himself over and over again through His works?

> *The works of his hands are verity and judgment; all his commandments are sure. They stand fast for ever and ever, and are done in truth and uprightness. He sent redemption unto his people: he hath commanded his covenant for ever: holy and reverend is his name* (Psalm 111:7-9).

> *For the LORD giveth wisdom: out of his mouth cometh knowledge and under-standing* (Proverbs 2:6).

But let us start out our quest for wisdom with the right attitude, and that is godly and reverential fear. Proverbs 9:10 says, "The *fear* of the *LORD* is the *beginning* of *wisdom*, and *knowledge* of the *Holy* One is *understanding*" and Psalm 110:7-10 adds: "*The fear of the LORD is the beginning of wisdom: a good understanding have all they that do his commandments: his praise endureth for ever.*"

We are counted wise only when we fear the Lord, and have understanding of the Holy One. Now this is not the fear that causes us to be in terror of Him for making the slightest mistake. No, the fear of the Lord in this context is more of a reverential fear based on a continual awareness of Him, and a sincere commitment to obey Him.

So what are the rewards of finding wisdom?

Please consider the following scriptures:

A discerning and excellent spirit - Proverbs 17:27-28:

> *He that hath knowledge spareth his words: and a man of understanding is of an excellent spirit. Even a fool, when he holdeth his peace, is counted wise: and he that shutteth his lips is esteemed a man of understanding.*

Longevity - Proverbs 9:10:

*For by me thy days shall be multiplied,
and the years of thy life shall be increased.*

Longevity, happiness, pleasantness, prosperity, honor, peace, abundant life – Proverbs 3:13-18:

Happy is the man that findeth wisdom, and the man that getteth understanding. For the merchandise of it is better than the merchandise of silver, and the gain thereof than fine gold. She is more precious than rubies: and all the things thou canst desire are not to be compared unto her. Length of days is in her right hand; and in her left hand riches and honour. Her ways are ways of pleasantness, and all her paths are peace. She is a tree of life to them that lay hold upon her: and happy is every one that retaineth her.

All the fruit of the Holy Spirit on display - James 3:17:

> *But the wisdom that is from above is first*
> *pure, then peaceable, gentle, and easy to*
> *be intreated, full of mercy and good fruits,*
> *without partiality, and without hypocrisy.*

There are no earthly possessions or jewels worthy of being compared with the truth of who He is. No precious jewels or earthly treasures can compare with true wisdom. We must make wisdom our business; we must venture totally in it and be willing to part with all for it.

Matthew Henry in his Commentary on wisdom says the following:

> "No precious jewels or earthly treasures are worthy to be compared with true wisdom, whether the concerns of time or eternity be considered. We must make wisdom our business; we must venture all in it, and be willing to part with all for it. This Wisdom is the Lord Jesus Christ and His salvation, sought and obtained by faith and prayer. Were it not for unbelief, remaining sinfulness, and carelessness, we should find all our ways

pleasantness, and our paths peace, for His are so; but we too often step aside from them, to our own hurt and grief."

On the other hand, those that reject wisdom lack the fear of the Lord. The Bible considers such people fools. So, while the fear of the LORD is the beginning of knowledge, *"fools despise wisdom and instruction"* (Proverbs 1:7). The Bible goes on to say that such people are not only foolish, they are corrupt. Their future is devoid of promise, for ultimately they will be given over to a reprobate or degenerate mind:

> *The fool hath said in his heart, There is no God. They are corrupt, they have done abominable works, there is none that doeth good* (Psalm 14:1).

> *And even as they did not like to retain God in their knowledge, God gave them over to a reprobate mind, to do those things which are not convenient* (Romans 8:1:28).

Tool #3

Faith

In our Christian walk everything we do must come from faith, for the Bible says, *"The just shall live by faith"* (Romans 1:17).

What is faith?

Hebrews 11:1, says, *"Now faith is the substance of things hoped for, the evidence of things not seen."*

How do we obtain faith? There is only one way: by grace.

> *For by grace are ye saved through faith;*
> *and that not of yourselves: it is the gift of*
> *God* (Ephesians 2:8).

Why did God give us the gift of faith? It's the channel He uses to bring us to salvation – salvation to be born again and on-going salvation for our sanctification.

What is the guarantee of our faith?

The Holy Spirit is the guarantor of our faith. It is because of what Jesus Christ did on the cross that solidifies this for us.

> *Having believed, you were marked in him with a seal, the promised Holy Spirit, who is a deposit guaranteeing our inheritance until the redemption of those who are God's possession – to the praise of his glory* (Ephesians 1:13-14).

Is faith something I can earn?

No, it is a gift, *"Not of works, lest any man should boast"* (Ephesians 2:9). God deserves all the glory for our salvation. Since it is given freely as a gift, we can be assured of it despite our sinful nature. Since we can do nothing to earn it, we have no right to boast in it. We are to walk in humility and not to think more highly of ourselves that we should.

How is the amount of faith we are given decided? Is it based on merit?

Only God can decide on the measure of faith we are given based on His reckoning.

For I say, through the grace given unto me, to every man that is among you, not to think of himself more highly than he ought to think; but to think soberly, according as God hath dealt to every man the measure of faith (Romans 12:3).

Who would have thought these words could have come from Paul, a former persecutor of Christians? On the way to Damascus to arrest more Christians he had a dramatic encounter with the Lord and was struck blind. From there, he received his eyesight, both in the natural and spiritual, and the faith to have his whole life transformed (see Acts 9).

How do we develop faith?

The bible identifies the course of action and the method He used to secure saving faith in His people. It comes from hearing the Word of God for it is the Word of God that produces faith. Any time the true gospel is heard it is the fertile soil for producing faith.

What can I do to receive from God?

We must first believe without doubting before we can expect to receive anything from Him.

> *But let him ask in faith, nothing wavering. For he that wavereth is like a wave of the sea driven with the wind and tossed. For let not that man think that he shall receive any thing of the Lord* (James 1:7).

How can we come to please Him?

Again, we can only please Him through faith.

> *But without faith it is impossible to please him: for he that cometh to God must believe that he is, and that he is a rewarder of them that diligently seek him* (James 1:6-7).

How do we become sons of God?

When we receive Jesus Christ as our Lord and Savior through faith, we become His sons. If we used to bear the DNA of Adam when we were born, we bear the DNA of Christ when we are born again.

> *But as many as received him, to them gave he power to become the **sons** of God, even to them that believe on his name: Which were born, not of blood, nor of the will of the flesh, nor of the will of man, but of God (John 1:12-13, emphasis added).*

In the above verse, the Greek word used to express "sons" is *tekna,* which more properly refers to "children." But the New Testament sometimes makes a distinction between *tekna* and *huios* to contrast "children" with "sons" in terms of maturity and growth.

> *"For the earnest expectation of the creature waiteth for the manifestation of the sons of God"* (Romans 8:19). Here the Greek word for "sons" is derived from *huios* and speaks of maturity. So, once

saved, as we continue to live a life of faith, we can count ourselves as maturing into sons of God.

What is required to do the work of God?

This was the question raised by the Pharisees in an attempt to challenge Him.

Then said they unto him, What shall we do, that we might work the works of God?

Jesus answered and said unto them, This is the work of God, that ye believe on him whom he hath sent.

They said therefore unto him, What sign shewest thou then, that we may see, and believe thee? what dost thou work? Our fathers did eat manna in the desert; as it is written, He gave them bread from heaven to eat.

Then Jesus said unto them, Verily, verily, I say unto you, Moses gave you not that bread from heaven; but my Father giveth you the true bread from heaven. For the bread of God is he which cometh down from heaven, and giveth life unto the world.

Then said they unto him, Lord, evermore give us this bread.

And Jesus said unto them, I am the bread of life: he that cometh to me shall never hunger; and he that believeth on me shall never thirst (Matthew 6:28-35).

The Pharisees asked for a sign from Him. In other words, they were trying to get Him to perform for them to prove He was the Son of God. They were saying, "Once we see what You work, then we will decide if we will believe," trying to put Jesus on a merit system to decide whether they believed or not.

For Jesus, however, there was only one requirement: that they believe on Him whom God had sent. However, their security and trust were in Moses. Even in their so-called state of security, He revealed to them that the bread of true significance was the bread of life that came from the Father (verse 32). It is vested in a Person: Himself.

> *For the bread of God is he which cometh down from heaven, and giveth life unto the world. Then said they unto him, Lord, evermore give us this bread. And Jesus said unto them, I am the bread of life: he that cometh to me shall never hunger; and he that believeth on me shall never thirst (Matthew 6:34-35).*

What is the message of faith all about?

The good news of the Gospel of Jesus Christ. Hearing about Him is the avenue to faith and salvation. The scripture says,

> *How then shall they call on him in whom they have not believed? and how shall they believe in him of whom they have not heard? and how shall they hear without a preacher? And how shall they preach,*

except they be sent? as it is written, how beautiful are the feet of them that preach the gospel of peace and bring glad tidings of good things! But they have not all obeyed the gospel. For Esaias saith, Lord, who hath believed our report? So, then **faith cometh by hearing, and hearing by the word of God** (Romans 10:14-17, emphasis added).

This is why the carrying out of the great commission is so vital. In it we are proclaiming Jesus Christ and what He has so graciously secured for humanity. It is not produced by the eloquence of man's speech or the perfection of his sermon or the impressiveness of his theology. It is not determined by the display or the accuracy of a man's gift. It is the simple message about Jesus Christ that develops God ordained faith.

Can I ask God for more faith?

Yes, you can. *"And the apostles said unto the Lord, Increase our faith"* (Luke 17:5)

How is faith perfected?

It is through God who is the author and finisher of our faith.

> *Looking unto Jesus the **author and fin-isher** of our faith, who for the joy that was set before him endured the cross, despising the shame, and is set down at the right hand of the throne of God* (Hebrews 12:2, emphasis added).

If it's a gift does this mean I do not have to do anything to cultivate my faith?

Well, look at how Paul instructs Timothy in 2 Timothy 1:6 to "stir up the gifts." All the gifts can and will become dormant if we do not use them, and faith is one of them. Once true faith is acquired, this kind of faith gains mastery over human perception, over sickness and disease, over defeat and the kingdom of darkness. It brings us into great power for service: to heal the sick, to cast out devils, to do all manner of miracles, signs and wonders. Jesus said,

> *Verily, verily, I say unto you, He that be-*
> *lieveth on me, the works that I do shall*
> *he do also; and greater works than these*
> *shall he do; because I go unto my Father*
> (John 14:2).

On our part, we must cultivate our faith. We must do our due diligence to nurture and bring it to full maturity. We must painstakingly endeavor to continue in a posture until it is complete. This also entails welcoming all opportunities to increase our faith, so that we can believe enough to contend for the kind of faith that was once delivered to the Saints. Let us do as the Apostle Jude says:

> *Beloved, when I gave all diligence to write*
> *unto you of the common salvation, it was*
> *needful for me to write unto you, and ex-*
> *hort you that ye should earnestly contend*
> *for the faith which was once delivered*
> *unto the saints* (Jude 1:3).

Let us continue to exercise our faith as we fulfill the command of Jesus in His parting words before He ascended to heaven.

And he said unto them, Go ye into all the world, and preach the gospel to every creature. He that believeth and is baptized shall be saved; but he that believeth not shall be damned. And these signs shall follow them that believe; In my name shall they cast out devils; they shall speak with new tongues; They shall take up serpents; and if they drink any deadly thing, it shall not hurt them; they shall lay hands on the sick, and they shall recover. So then after the Lord had spoken unto them, he was received up into heaven, and sat on the right hand of God. And they went forth, and preached every where, the Lord working with them, and confirming the word with signs following. Amen (Mark 16:14-22).

Prayer

What is prayer?

Prayer is the direct communication between a person and the one who created that person, the Lord.

What is the purpose of prayer?

It's communication with God the Father. It is the primary way to share our heart, feelings emotions and desires and to receive His direction. It is also the source He uses through us to bring about His will on the earth.

How are we to pray?

All prayer must be offered in faith. When we pray, we are to address and acknowledge the Father, and petition Him in the name of our Lord and Savior Jesus Christ, while asking the Holy Spirit to guide us.

How did Jesus instruct us to pray?

Jesus provides for us the guidelines and perfect model for prayer. This is recorded for our learning in Matthew 6 and Luke 11. Luke gives great emphasis to the Lord's prayer life, for the disciples noticed that He often stole away to meet with the Father in prayer. This enabled them to see that prayer was essential and to want Him to teach them as John the Baptist taught his disciples.

It is imperative that we take on the meaning and the understanding of why we are to pray and why this kind of a prayer is important. Matthew 6 and Luke 11 show three components of His prayer that are the essential framework of His model prayer.

1. How to pray (Matthew 6:9-13)

> *After this manner therefore pray ye: Our*
> *Father which art in heaven, Hallowed be*
> *thy name. Thy kingdom come, Thy will be*

done in earth, as it is in heaven. Give us
this day our daily bread. And forgive us
our debts, as we forgive our debtors. And
lead us not into temptation, but deliver us
from evil: For thine is the kingdom, and
the power, and the glory, for ever. Amen.

The first part of the prayer extols the name of God and the Kingdom of God. It acknowledges the rulership of the Father being fully established here on earth, and for His Glory and Splendor to be revealed. The next section of the prayer deals with our physical needs, for God our Father is also the provider for His children. We are taught to seek Him for all that is essential for our physical needs. We also ask Him for forgiveness of our sins, so the barrier of sin between us is removed, and we place ourselves under His protection from committing future sins. And as we are forgiven, so also do we forgive others who have offended us. It should be our desire to not be tempted. God allows us to deal with sin at the root rather than to wait for it to display its fruit. We close the prayer in expectation of God's Kingdom, along with the manifestation of His Power and Glory.

However, if this prayer is simply recited without understanding, it becomes nothing but vain repetition. We may not pray the exact words of the Lord's prayer, but we should pray along the lines of it. When we do not pray for His name to be hallowed and for His Kingdom to come, we are in danger of cultivating a love for the world with no desire to see it replaced by the righteous reign of God. When we do not pray for our daily bread from Him, we display a self-sufficient attitude which does not depend upon God's daily provision. When we fail to pray for His forgiveness along with the grace to forgive others, we are either in denial or our conscience is seared by sin, for a conscience steeped in sin does not seek forgiveness.

2. Pray with persistence (Luke 11:5-8)

> *And he said unto them, Which of you*
> *shall have a friend, and shall go unto him*
> *at midnight, and say unto him, Friend,*
> *lend me three loaves; For a friend of mine*
> *in his journey is come to me, and I have*
> *nothing to set before him? And he from*
> *within shall answer and say, Trouble me*

not: the door is now shut, and my children are with me in bed; I cannot rise and give thee. I say unto you, Though he will not rise and give him, because he is his friend, yet because of his importunity he will rise and give him as many as he needeth.

The man in need boldly, shamelessly, and persistently compels his friend to get up in the middle of the night to open the door and give him what he requests even though it was highly inconvenient. How much more will our Heavenly Father give to us His children!

3. Ask for the Holy Spirit (Luke 11:9-13)

And I say unto you, Ask, and it shall be given you; seek, and ye shall find; knock, and it shall be opened unto you. For every one that asketh receiveth; and he that seeketh findeth; and to him that knocketh it shall be opened. If a son shall ask bread of any of you that is a father, will he give him a stone? or if he ask a fish, will he for a fish give him a serpent? Or if he shall ask an egg, will he offer him a scorpion? If ye then, being evil, know how to give good gifts unto your children: how much more shall your heavenly Father give the Holy Spirit to them that ask him?

Jesus instructs the disciples when they pray to God to see Him as their Father, who delights in giving good gifts to His children. Human fathers do not give bad or harmful gifts to their children, so how much more should we expect good things of our Heavenly Father. The highest good for mankind, apart from salvation, is wrapped in His gift of the Holy Spirit. What better gift can the Lord give to those who are His!

Holy Living

To be holy means to be set apart or separate from evil and sin. God is holy. He is completely detached from sin and all manner of evil. When we walk in the light and seek God's repentance, He will cleanse us of all sin.

> *This then is the message which we have heard of him, and declare unto you, that God is light, and in him is no darkness at all. If we say that we have fellowship with him, and walk in darkness, we lie, and do not the truth: But if we walk in the light, as he is in the light, we have fellowship one with another, and the blood of Jesus Christ his Son cleanseth us from all sin. If we say that we have no sin, we deceive ourselves, and the truth is not in us* (1 John 1:5-8).

The beginning of holiness for the believer is walking in obedience to His word. *"For as by one man's disobedience many were made sinners, so by the obedience of one shall many be made righteous"* (Romans 5:19). So the first step towards holiness is accepting Christ as our Lord and Savior. Once this happens, we are made right and just before God by our faith: *"Therefore being justified by faith, we have peace with God through our Lord Jesus Christ"* (Romans 5:1).

We are commanded to be holy just as He is Holy. *"Be ye holy; for I am holy"* (1 Peter 1:16). We can only do this through the power of the Holy Spirit. Outside of the work of the Holy Spirit it is not possible for any Christian to be holy. *"Not by might, nor by power, but by my spirit, saith the LORD of hosts"* (Zechariah 4:6). That requires that we have the Holy Spirit indwelling us to constantly fill us.

Although it is not always easy to choose the path to obedience, it is possible if our will does not block us. We overcome temptation by continuing in the Word of God. During times of temptation the way of escape provided for us is obedience to His word.

We are to live holy and clean lives for the Glory of God to be revealed in us to the world around us. We must remain in righteousness; if not, Satan will mock us. We must walk in the Spirit, so we will not desire to fulfill the lusts of the flesh. We must endeavor to live pure lives so that His character may be seen in us that men may see our good works and glorify God.

Ye are the salt of the earth: but if the salt has lost his savour, wherewith shall it be salted? it is thenceforth good for nothing, but to be cast out, and to be trodden under foot of men. Ye are the light of the world. A city that is set on a hill cannot be hid. Neither do men light a candle, and put it under a bushel, but on a candlestick; and it giveth light unto all that are in the house. Let your light so shine before men, that they may see your good works, and glorify your Father which is in heaven (Matthew 5:13-16).

To walk in holiness is to be liberated from the yoke of sin. Disobedience to His words brings us into bondage under Satan's rule and domain. The Holy Spirit will produce the Christ-like nature in us as we continue to yield to Him. We must count ourselves dead to sin and disobedience when it rears its head through temptation. We are to remind ourselves that we are dead to the flesh but alive to God in Christ Jesus. We must renew our minds at each moment to remind ourselves it was a part of our old nature. Choose to exercise the fruit of the Spirit that speaks to the temptation, for example, show kindness when confronted with nastiness, and endurance when we encounter delays. See yourself clothed in the righteousness of Christ Jesus.

At the same time, our quest for holiness must not in any way be thought of as the means to earn salvation or holiness. The spiritual fruit in our lives is by God's grace and being filled with the Holy Spirit. When we make a mistake, we must pick ourselves up, confess our sins, and continue in the righteousness of God in Christ Jesus.

> *There is therefore now no condemnation to them which are in Christ Jesus, who walk not after the flesh, but after the Spirit. For the law of the Spirit of life in*

Christ Jesus hath made me free from the law of sin and death. For what the law could not do, in that it was weak through the flesh, God sending his own Son in the likeness of sinful flesh, and for sin, condemned sin in the flesh: That the righteousness of the law might be fulfilled in us, who walk not after the flesh, but after the Spirit (Romans 8:1-4).

Lord, empty our will and heart so we may yield and surrender in all areas. Take away the appetites, motives, identity, intentions, false belief systems and their strongholds. It is only with a new heart that we can genuinely love You. You assure us that Your grace is sufficiently designed for our every weakness. Thank You that where we do not meet the measuring rod, You become the rod and the measure. All things are met in You.

To be filled with Him, we must be empty vessels. The scripture says you cannot put old wine into a new wineskin because the old has reached its full capacity to contain the wine. New wine, which is still fermenting and expanding, needs a new wineskin. With it comes flexibility, that is, the capacity to be stretched and to hold. The self-nature with its guile aims to keep us full of the flesh, and resist the infilling of the Holy Spirit. It is opposed to the Christ-like nature. This means we must take up our cross each day to die to sin and its nature. The one who loses their life daily is the one who will find their life in Christ. He that loses the flesh-filled life will gain the Christ-filled life. Loyalty to self will keep us bound to the inbred nature and open us to all the onslaughts of the enemy. Let us be crucified with Christ today and live, not as we would wish, but as He would through us.

We are to take the yoke of Christ upon us and learn of Him. For His burden is light and His yoke is easy. Here you will find rest for your souls. Life becomes simple without the need for the theatrics of the flesh life. One of two things will happen each day: I will either be led by the Spirit and follow the path of peace and walk in obedience or I will walk in disobedience and suffer the aftermath of torment and intrusion. It truly is that simple.

Obedience is perfected through suffering in the same way that Christ learned obedience through the things He suffered. In His completion of death by crucifixion, He completed the process required for obedience to God. Obedience to God was completed by His death on the cross. The psalmist David expressed gratitude for being afflicted so that he could come to know the laws and statutes of God and learn how to please Him (Psalm 19:7-11).

We must love Him more than all the things required for fulfilling the self-life. The struggle is in putting aside what you love and not giving in to our fleshly desires. In this we must empty out ourselves for love of Him. If not, we will do what is contrary to His Will. We must give all our fears, desires, appetites, and concerns over to Him, for he that loses his life will gain it. All that is required is to follow Christ. He is the one who knows what the "all that is required" truly is. He alone knows the human heart with all its deceitfulness.

Anything left alive in the will or appetite is still a part of the sin nature. It becomes one of the temptations not only of the flesh but also of the appetites that cause us to sin against God. We must not be deceived by the flesh and have no loyalty to it, for the flesh wars against the Spirit and the Spirit against the flesh. All of this is compounded by satanic powers aiming to block not only the plan of God, but the Glory of God revealed in us. We must take off all labor, for it is not in works. It is only by the Spirit of God. Not by power nor by might but only by His Spirit will He create both the will and the ability to do all His good pleasure in us.

This truly is an inward battle. It is won or lost in the Spirit. We will only overcome the flesh and the world by walking in the Spirit.

> *Walk in the Spirit, and ye shall not fulfill the lust of the flesh. For the flesh lusteth against the Spirit, and the Spirit against the flesh: these are contrary to the other so that ye cannot do the things that ye would* (Galatians 5:16).

We take on His will, His nature, His mind, His desires, His beliefs and values, His appetites, His deeds, His feelings, His senses, His character, and identity. The key to overcoming happens when you no longer seek to fulfill the desires of the flesh, and when you no longer seek to bring about satisfaction to the flesh with its lusts, passions, and appetites.

However, be assured that for every temptation He will create a way for us to escape it if it is truly our desire. What is the escape and how will it appear to us? It will appear in the form of His word, in a song or scripture, even being reminded of something spoken to you. When it is revealed, we must take the escape route provided for us, which is obedience to His word. To be prepared and on guard we must understand how temptations affect us and their inner workings in our lives. We must know our weaknesses to fortify ourselves against the traps and pitfalls awaiting us from Satan. We need to identify them when they come, and know how our thought life gave rise to such temptations.

What are the things that emanate from the heart? Check and be aware of feelings and emotions. These all play a huge role in overcoming. If I can determine the cause, I am no longer ignorant of Satan's devices. The word of God reveals all the stratagems of the enemy. The Lord wants us to be vigilant and on guard. We must be ready to be emptied, filled, and sealed with the Glory of God. When you come to a place of understanding, seek the things from above for total completeness of spirit, soul, and body.

> *If ye then be risen with Christ, seek those things which are above, where Christ sitteth on the right hand of God* (Colossians 3:1).

> *For whatsoever is born of God overcometh the world: this is the victory that overcometh the world, even our faith* (John 5:4).

We must take a moment to ask ourselves a few questions to define the state of our true inner selves.

What are your true desires? (secret life)

What is your quest in life?

What do you believe about God? (your inner belief system)

What governs your desires, habits, and appetites?

What are your motives and drive? (hidden agenda)

What will you do to get what you want or desire, and how far will you go to get it?

The corrupt nature is set to prohibit and hinder us from walking in the Spirit; this is defined here as the carnal mind. *"Because the carnal mind is enmity against God: for it is not subject to the law of God, neither indeed can be"* (Romans 8:7). A carnal mind is set against God's moral and His Spiritual laws, and it does not cherish the things of God; neither can it because it is in constant enmity with the law of God.

We can overcome the works of the flesh or the sinful nature by partaking of the goodness of God through the death of His Son. By the work of His precious Holy Spirit, we can once again receive that innate ability to enjoy the Christ-life nature within us. In this, the Holy Spirit will fashion Himself in the life of the one who will surrender all to Him. He will come and abide with this one to make for Himself a dwelling place, and a homestead.

Patience

What is patience?

There are two Greek words translated as "patience" in the New Testament. *Hupomonē* means "a remaining under" as when one bears up under a burden. It refers to steadfastness in difficult circumstances. Then there is *makrothumia,* as used in Galatians 5:22, which is a compound formed by *makros* ("long") and *thumos* ("passion" or "temper"). So "patience" in Galatians 5:22 literally means "long temper" (as against "short temper") or "the ability to hold one's temper for a long time." The KJV translates it as "longsuffering."

The Bible uses patience in both senses depending on the context. In addition to the simple use of the word "patience," when it comes to suffering, the word "longsuffering" is sometimes used, or when it comes to continuing through adversity, the word "enduring" may also be used. The opposite of patience is agitation, discouragement, and a desire for revenge.

As one of the fruit of the Spirit, patience then is a product of self-control and godliness, as demonstrated by Jesus. Patience is an important part of helping us grow and become stronger in our faith during trials. Our patience pleases God and results in His blessing. The lack of patience demonstrates ungodly thinking devoid of the protection and knowledge of God. Giving into impatience is a sign of weakness and leads to injustice and unmerciful treatment of others.

Trying situations teach us patience because hope is produced, which gives us the ability to endure suffering and tribulation.

> *For we are saved by hope: but hope that is seen is not hope: for what a man seeth, why doth he yet hope for? But if we hope for that we see not, then do we with patience wait for it* (Romans 8:24-25).

When we are patient, He is glorified and is able to work within our hearts and through our situations in life, even in our relationships. What are the characteristics of a patient person? A patient person can endure much pain and suffering without complaint. A patient person is slow to anger as he waits for God to provide comfort and punish wrongdoing. Since patience is a fruit of the Spirit, we can only possess *makrothumia* through the Holy Spirit at work in us.

We can choose to be patient with a vexatious person who has lost all compassion. Nevertheless, we love that person and continue to desire the best for them. This reflects the character of God, who shows infinite patience towards sinners, waiting for the time they respond to His offer of salvation.

> *The Lord is not slack concerning his promise, as some men count slackness; but is longsuffering to us-ward, not willing that any should perish, but that all should come to repentance* (2 Peter 3:9).

Testing and Trials

There is far more to testing and trials than one can ever fathom. God allows them as a refining process in the life of the believer. Some trials come to test and to purify our faith. Other times God will allow them to prepare us for promotion. So, rest assured, each test or trial is governed by a divine plan and has a purpose in your life.

The Message Bible puts it this way,

> *Consider it a sheer gift, friends, when tests and challenges come at you from all sides. You know that under pressure, your faith-life is forced into the open and shows its true colors. So don't try to get out of anything prematurely. Let it do its work, so you become mature and well-developed, not deficient in any way* (James 1:1-4).

Although I have not ever had a test or trial that I was thrilled to see, at the end of the day I found myself grateful for them. Testing and trials are necessary for our spiritual learning and the development of our faith.

> *So be truly glad. There is wonderful joy ahead, even though you must endure many trials for a little while. These trials*

will show that your faith is genuine. It is being tested as fire tests and purifies gold—though your faith is far more precious than mere gold. So when your faith remains strong through many trials, it will bring you much praise and glory and honor on the day when Jesus Christ is revealed to the whole world. You love him even though you have never seen him. Though you do not see him now, you trust him; and you rejoice with a glorious, inexpressible joy (1 Peter 1:6-8 NLT).

Therefore see patience as a valuable commodity in your life. It is the process along with the trials and tribulations that bring about all the perfect work of Christ in our lives.

James encourages us in our trials with this radical statement:

My brethren, count it all joy when ye fall into divers temptations; Knowing this, that the trying of your faith worketh patience. But let patience have her perfect work, that ye may be perfect and entire, wanting nothing ...

Wherefore, my beloved brethren, let every man be swift to hear, slow to speak, slow to wrath: For the wrath of man worketh not the righteousness of God. Wherefore lay apart all filthiness and superfluity of naughtiness, and receive with meekness the engrafted word, which is able to save your souls (James 1:2-3; 19-21).

For patience must have her perfect work in the life of each person. It takes us from the place of desiring to have the likeness of Christ to the actuality of becoming more like Christ. Patience gets us there by faith. She understands time is her most essential component for her work to come to perfection but she is not in a hurry regardless of how difficult the suffering. Her goal is to fashion each one with the desires of Christ, to be emptied, and on completion, to be entire and to lack no good thing.

The Power of Words

Before we go into the spoken "word" and the power it stores, we must first show its connection with God. We must first establish that God is who He says He is and speaks. The God of the Bible calls Himself *Elohim* (the triune God) or *Yehovah* (the I am). This is who is He. What is the key characteristic of this God?

Isaiah 42:8 paints a vivid picture of one key characteristic:

> *I am the* Lord: *that is my name: and my glory will I not give to another, neither my praise to graven images.*

Let us examine some key words here. Now when the word LORD appears in capital letters, it denotes the Hebrew word for His name, which is generally *Yehovah* or *Jehovah*. The literal meaning is "I am the one who is" or simply "I am." God identified Himself to Moses from the burning bush as *"I Am That I Am: and he* said, *Thus shalt thou say unto the children of Israel, I Am hath sent me unto you* (Exodus 3:14). The Hebrew word for "glory" is *kabod*, meaning "weight," "splendor," "glory" or "honor, while "praise" comes from the Hebrew word *tehillah.*

So we know that *Yehovah* will not give the praise and honor due Him to anyone – not angels, demons, men or idols. That means human beings must not take on for themselves any glory for gifts or talents, ideas, doctrine, works, wisdom, power, or ability that has come from God. They are all for His glory. Man is not worthy of such glory: how much less are images worthy of it?

> *Thou art worthy, O Lord, to receive glory and honour and power: for thou hast created all things, and for thy pleasure they are and were created* (Revelation 3:11).

> *For by him were all things created, that are in heaven, and that are in earth, visible and invisible, whether they be thrones, or dominions, or principalities, or powers: all things were created by him, and for*

him: And he is before all things, and by him all things consist (Colossians 1:16-17).

How does God speak to us?

He uses mainly the spoken word to communicate with us, although visions and dreams may be part of the medium. Whatever the means, they convey the "Word" of His Son Jesus Christ who speaks to us according to Hebrews 1:1-3:

> *God, who at sundry times and in divers manners spake in time past unto the fathers by the prophets, Hath in these last days spoken unto us by his Son, whom he hath appointed heir of all things, by whom also he made the worlds; Who being the brightness of his glory, and the express image of his person, and upholding all things by the word of his power, when he had by himself purged our sins, sat down on the right hand of the Majesty on high.*

His voice can be audible, and it can be heard in a language known to the hearer. For all language is from Him. He has power over words, language and speech. *"In the beginning was the Word, and the Word was with God, and the Word was God"* (John 1:1). The Word, Jesus Christ, is God and all words originate from God; the Creator of our universe, our lives, our reality.

Now we see in Genesis 11 how the people of the earth originally spoke one language and had one speech. But look what happened when that civilization rose up to take the glory of God for themselves:

> *And the whole earth was of one language, and of one speech. And it came to pass, as they journeyed from the east, that they found a plain in the land of Shinar; and they dwelt there. And they said one to another, Go to, let us make brick, and burn them thoroughly. And they had brick for stone, and slime had they for mortar. And they said, Go to, let us build us a city and a tower, whose top may reach unto heaven; and **let us make us a name**, lest*

we be scattered abroad upon the face of the whole earth.

*And the Lord came down to see the city and the tower, which the children of men builded. And the Lord said, Behold, the people is one, and they have all one language; and this they begin to do: and **now nothing will be restrained from them**, which they have imagined to do. Go to, let us go down, and there confound their language, that they may not understand one another's speech. So the Lord scattered them abroad from thence upon the face of all the earth: and they left off to build the city. Therefore is the name of it called Babel; because the Lord did there confound the language of all the earth: and from thence did the Lord scatter them abroad upon the face of all the earth* (Genesis 11:2-5; 7-9, emphasis added).

This is a reminder to us when we attempt to misappropriate the glory that belongs solely to God. God not only confounded their speech, but He also scattered them across the earth. Interestingly, the name "Babel" means "a confused sound of many voices." So God put them into disarray by bringing confusion to their speech and breaking up their unity to rule themselves without His name.

Contrast this disunity in rebellion with the spirit of unity in the upper room on the day of Pentecost.

> *And when the day of Pentecost was fully come, they were all with **one accord** in one place. And suddenly there came a sound from heaven as of a rushing mighty wind, and it filled all the house where they were sitting. And there appeared unto them cloven tongues like as of fire, and it sat upon each of them. And they were all filled with the Holy Ghost, and began to speak with other tongues, as the Spirit gave them utterance.*
>
> *And there were dwelling at Jerusalem Jews, devout men, out of every nation under heaven. Now when this was noised*

abroad, the multitude came together, and were confounded, because that every man heard them speak in his own language. And they were all amazed and marvelled, saying one to another, Behold, are not all these which speak Galilaeans? And how hear we every man in our own tongue, wherein we were born? Parthians, and Medes, and Elamites, and the dwellers in Mesopotamia, and in Judaea, and Cappadocia, in Pontus, and Asia, Phrygia, and Pamphylia, in Egypt, and in the parts of Libya about Cyrene, and strangers of Rome, Jews and proselytes, Cretes and Arabians, we do hear them speak in our tongues the wonderful works of God. And they were all amazed, and were in doubt, saying one to another, What meaneth this? (Acts 1-12)

We can vividly see the power of unity when it's a unity in praise of His wonderful works. Even more so, we see God's power over speech and language, causing the disciples to speak in other tongues, in this case, in languages unknown to them but known to the hearers from other lands. He confounded one group and unified another according to the condition of the heart of each group of people, for He had full control of language.

Who can hear His voice? He that has an ear to hear and recognizes the voice of God. His sheep will hear His voice because they know His voice, and the voice of a stranger they will not follow (John 10:4-5). Who are the sheep? Those that make Jesus Christ their Lord and Savior, that have become familiar with His voice and His Word, and that consistently tune their ears to listen out for Him amid the babble of voices around. We know and are assured His voice will never speak contrary to His Word.

And, because Jesus is alive, His Word has a voice. God speaks to us audibly and to our spirit through the Word, and the Holy Spirit. Jesus tells us that our words too are alive and reach into the spirit realm: *"It is the Spirit that quickeneth, the flesh profiteth nothing: the words that I speak unto you, they are Spirit, and they are life"* (John 6:63) just as 1 Timothy 4:1 states, *"the Spirit speaks expressly..."* about the times we are in.

What else is important other than having a hearing ear? Faith. Faith is required for us to embrace the biblical account of creation. *"Through faith we understand that the worlds were framed by the word of God, so that things which are seen were not made of things which do appear"* (Hebrews 11:3). By faith we accept what the Bible says about creation and not what the scientists and evolutionists would have us believe.

Let us now explore the meaning of "word" in secular terms. The Merriam-Webster dictionary defines "word" as a sound or combination of sounds that has *meaning* and is spoken by a human being," or "a written or printed letter or letters standing for a spoken *word*." Spoken words consist of vibrations and sounds, which when combined together, create our world. Without such a meaningful combination, a thought can never become a reality. Our words and thoughts are therefore the tools we use to shape our reality. Similarly, the written word conveys our thoughts through meaningful written symbols. If our words can create our reality, this means they have energy and power when released. They have the ability to help, to heal and build up, on the one hand, as well as to hinder, to hurt, to harm, to humiliate and humble, on the other.

If we dissect the spoken word in our word life, that is, the words that proceed out of our mouth, we will discover that much of the content is from our internal dialogue. How we allow that dialogue to play in our minds, and what comes out in speech is the natural fruit of what proceeds from our hearts. Jesus says, *"Out of the abundance of the heart the mouth speaketh"* (Luke 6:45). Therefore take charge of the words that issue out of your mouth and the thoughts you allow to penetrate your mind, for the fruit of it will be your reward.

Even if we choose not to accept this truth, the principle still remains. We frame our lives by the words we use. We must learn to put a guard at the door of our lips; if not, it will rob us of the peace and blessings promised by God. We are what we think, for as a man thinks in his heart, so is he. We can choose to use our words to speak doom and destruction not only in our own lives but also in the lives of our family, friends, community, leaders and nation. Or we can choose our words to build up and bring life.

Death and life are in the power of the tongue: and they that love it shall eat the fruit thereof (Proverbs 18:21).

The words of the wicked are to lie in wait for blood: but the mouth of the upright shall deliver them (Proverbs 11:6).

Here is a sober reminder of the power of the tongue:

But the tongue can no man tame; it is an unruly evil, full of deadly poison. Therewith bless we God, even the Father; and therewith curse we men, which are made after the similitude of God (James 3:8).

But first of all, let us guard our thought life. Jesus during a discourse with the Jews questions the kind of fruit that can come out of an evil heart:

O generation of vipers, how can ye, being evil, speak good things? for out of the abundance of the heart the mouth speaketh. A good man out of the good treasure

> *of the heart bringeth forth good things:*
> *and an evil man out of the evil trea-*
> *sure bringeth forth evil things* (Matthew
> 12:34-35).

With all these warnings, let us avoid gossip, slander, lying and loose talk, and be circumspect in what we say. In fact, our words are so important to God that we will have to give an account of what we say when we stand before Him.

> *But I say unto you, That every idle word*
> *that men shall speak, they shall give ac-*
> *count thereof in the day of judgment. For*
> *by thy words thou shalt be justified, and*
> *by thy words thou shalt be condemned*
> (Matthew 12:36-37).

And so, let us be renewed in the spirit of our mind and put off our negative inner dialogues and deceitful conversations as Paul advises:

> *... put off concerning the former con-*
> *versation the old man, which is corrupt*
> *according to the deceitful lusts; And be*

*renewed in the spirit of your mind; and
that ye put on the new man, which after
God is created in righteousness and true
holiness* (Ephesians 4:22-32).

Let us speak with grace, edifying and uplifting others:

*Let no corrupt communication proceed
out of your mouth, but that which is good
to the use of edifying, that it may minister
grace unto the hearers* (Ephesians 4:29).

Unwholesome communication has no place in the life of a Christian. Our speech is to be guided and directed only by what is helpful for building others up as is needed to benefit them.

*Let the word of Christ dwell in you richly
in all wisdom; teaching and admonishing
one another in psalms and hymns and
spiritual songs, singing with grace in your
hearts to the Lord* (Colossians 3:6).

> *Let your speech be always with grace, seasoned with salt, that ye may know how ye ought to answer every man* (Colossians 4:6).

In the same way, we are to stand on our faith and the power of our words when we petition God in prayer. *"And all things, whatsoever ye shall ask in prayer, believing, ye shall receive"* (Matthew 21:22).

We can therefore choose to be of the same mind as Him or we can choose to stand in the way of the sinner. Do we want to be in the company of those whose *"throat is an open sepulchre; with their tongues they have used deceit; the poison of asps is under their lips"* (Romans 3:13)? Certainly not! We want to be true worshipers of God and have the assurance that our prayers will be heard as Jesus promises in John 9:31: *"Now we know that God heareth not sinners: but if any man be a worshipper of God, and doeth his will, him he heareth."*

Here we see prayer that works. When our hearts are infused with the love of Christ, honesty, truth and purity will flow from our belly. Our hearts are to be set apart for Him in such a way we are always ready and willing to speak with gentleness and respect. Our words should exemplify the power of the grace of God and His indwelling Holy Spirit in our daily lives. Our hearts are changed by the power of God and our speech reflects His character.

A Sound Mind

All the forces in the universe are targeted at the human mind. In Genesis 2 and 3 we see two opposing forces arrayed for battle for the human mind. In Genesis 2, God sets His focus on the mind of Adam and Eve, outlining their responsibilities, and drawing boundaries for them.

> *And the LORD God took the man, and put him into the garden of Eden to dress it and to keep it. And the LORD God commanded the man, saying, Of every tree of the garden thou mayest freely eat: But of the tree of the knowledge of good and evil, thou shalt not eat of it: for in the day that thou eatest thereof thou shalt surely die* (Genesis 2:15-17).

This showed they were already intelligent, responsible beings with a conscience. The human mind is by design creative and imaginative and has the intrinsic ability to make rational choices, problem-solve and find solutions. There was already a moral imperative laid out. Human consciousness is at the root of the process of allowing us to function with ethics, justice, forgiveness, self-reproach, and love.

However, the mind needs to be trained by setting boundaries to it to know its limits and the consequences of deviant behavior. In Genesis 2, we see God setting boundaries and guidelines called ethics to Adam and Eve's mind. By contrast, in Genesis 3, we can see the Serpent promoting self-will through enticement and doubt in questioning the validity of what God plainly spoke. Here we see clearly how the serpent has aimed his tactics at disrupting their clarity of mind and undermining their belief system.

> *Now the serpent was more subtil than any beast of the field which the LORD God had made. And he said unto the woman, Yea, hath God said, Ye shall not eat of every tree of the garden?*
>
> *And the woman said unto the serpent, We may eat of the fruit of the trees of the*

garden: But of the fruit of the tree which is in the midst of the garden, God hath said, Ye shall not eat of it, neither shall ye touch it, lest ye die.

And the serpent said unto the woman, Ye shall not surely die: For God doth know that in the day ye eat thereof, then your eyes shall be opened, and ye shall be as gods, knowing good and evil (Genesis 3:1-5).

Since the fall of man, God had planned for the redemption of humanity to bring us back to the purity and order of Genesis 2. He enables us to return from a point of rejecting His ethics to acceptance of them. This He does through the redemption offered through His Son Jesus. We are all created to have an understanding of the workings of the human mind, for the Almighty gives us inspiration and understanding (Job 32:8). We are therefore accountable to God for how we use our minds. Only a proper understanding will bring us to self-evaluation and correction.

We are essentially made in the image of God and have an innate desire to conform to His nature. We can see His desire for us in His design since He created us in His image and likeness to have fellowship with Him. However, the thoughts of the natural man are swayed by both carnal and suggestive influences. This is a mindset that wars against the mind of Christ to lure us out of our boundaries. Why is it at enmity with God?

When Adam sinned, the God-given connection for man was lost and man became dominated by his senses – in a word – the carnal mind. The carnal mind refuses to be led by the Spirit of God or see the error of its ways. It will continue in this state of futility until it decides to change its perceptions. As long as it is in operation, it is impossible to please Him. However, embedded in us is still that inner quest or longing for the supernatural in all of us. It is what is missing in life apart from Him. We are not perfected until we are complete in Him. As Colossians 2:10 tells us, we are only complete in Him, the head of all principality and power.

This is what makes the Bible the most amazing story of Grace every told. It revolves entirely around humanity rejecting God, and then the provision for accepting Him as our Creator and Giver of sound minds. Only through the redeeming blood of Jesus, have our eyes been open to faith in Christ Jesus and the grace that abounds. It is God answering the powerful prayer of Paul in Ephesians 1:17-19:

> *… That the God of our Lord Jesus Christ, the Father of glory, may give unto you the spirit of wisdom and revelation in the knowledge of him: The eyes of your understanding being enlightened; that ye may know what is the hope of his calling, and what the riches of the glory of his inheritance in the saints, And what is the exceeding greatness of his power to us-ward who believe, according to the working of his mighty power.*

When we have made Jesus our Savior and Redeemer, we are new creations in Him. But the enemy will not give up and will continue to bombard our minds with his doubts and perverse thoughts. We must cooperate with the Holy Spirit in renewing our minds and resisting the onslaught of the enemy on our minds. Governing the "thought" life takes discipline and a life-long commitment. The devil's tactic is to infiltrate our thought life through the things we watch, our conversations and meditations. This is one area we must scrupulously guard, for the battleground is won or lost in the mind. How do we guard it?

> *Casting down imaginations, and every high thing that exalteth itself against the knowledge of God, and bringing into captivity every thought to the obedience of Christ* (2 Corinthians 10:5).

This calls for a strategic plan to master our thought life. We must bring every thought under subjection to the obedience of Christ and take every thought into captivity to arrest it. Put a guard on your mind, put on the helmet of salvation, create a band around your thought life, and institute restrictions and boundaries for the sake of the soundness and well-being of your mind.

What you meditate on and give thought to will be what you produce in life. For as a man thinks, so is he Proverbs 23:7. According to this principle, you become what you think. If our thoughts are this powerful and can produce this kind of a reality in my life, why do we not have the fruit of what we desire? I submit to you it's because we have been conditioned to accept and believe in the negative things in a society that fails to frame their lives based on the Word.

For the carnal mind will not ever desire to please the Lord. So is the state of any man who continues to walk in darkness. We must not be deceived by the "I just want to please the Lord" cliché we often use when really it is aimed at our own contentment. We want and need a powerful outpouring of His power at work in our lives, our families, government, our cities and this world. Let us take stock of our mind and thoughts more than our desire or the need for power or control, or to preserve what you have acquired. Only God can quench the longing of our souls.

But we who have the word of God hidden in our hearts know and apply Philippians 4:8 to our thought life:

> *Finally, brethren, whatsoever things are true, whatsoever things are honest, whatsoever things are just, whatsoever things are pure, whatsoever things are lovely, whatsoever things are of good report; if there be any virtue, and if there be any praise, think on these things.*

> And again, *"For as he thinketh in his heart, so is he"* (Psalm 23:7).

The things that you meditate on will govern your conscious and sub-conscious mind. What is it that you constantly meditate on? The doom and gloom from social media and predictions of shortages and disease outbreaks? These are so all pervasive, they can control your mind. But by an act of will, you can change the orientation of your mind by giving thanks to God for intervening in every situation. Philippians 4:6-7 says:

> *Be anxious for nothing, but in everything by prayer and supplication, with thanksgiving, let your requests be made known to God; and the peace of God, which surpasses all understanding, will guard your*

hearts and minds through Christ Jesus (NKJV).

Once you have cast your cares and anxieties unto God, leave them with Him. Just keep thanking Him, and soon His peace will come upon you. He promises you that peace as You trust Him for the solution even though you don't have any idea how it will happen. That is putting your faith in action. And we have His assurance He will keep those in perfect peace whose minds are stayed on Him (Isaiah 26:3). We must stop relinquishing our peace willingly to thoughts that trouble our minds and give rise to emotional and mental pain.

And again, what does Jesus say about worry and anxiety? He gives very practical advice. No amount of worry will change things you have little or no control over:

Which of you by taking thought can add one cubit unto his stature? (Matthew 4:4)

Therefore I say unto you, Take no thought for your life, what ye shall eat, or what ye shall drink; nor yet for your body, what ye shall put on. Is not the life more than meat, and the body than raiment? (Matthew 6:27)

Instead, put your priority on kingdom business and then everything you need will be added:

But seek ye first the kingdom of God, and his righteousness; and all these things shall be added unto you (Matthew 6:33).

Situations, times, and seasons do not determine the quality of our peace. All our dependence should be upon Jesus, the Prince of Peace. For He gives us the gift of peace – not an instability based on happenstance – but in spite of it. This is a guarantee regardless of what we experience in life. This is a promise we can come to depend on. With so much going on in the world, we can no longer have peace in the fluctuating economy or an uncertain retirement plan due to lack of integrity of our government or society. Only Jesus can give us unwavering peace.

*Peace I leave with you, my peace I give
unto you: not as the world giveth, give I
unto you. Let not your heart be troubled,
neither let it be afraid* (John 14:27).

We are equipped to keep our hearts with diligence, to understand where the residue of life is stored from what we encounter. The Bible refers to them as the issues of life, the corrupt nature, generational curses, or what life has dealt us due to our choices and decisions. *"Keep thy heart with all diligence, for out of it are the issues of life. Put away from thee a forward mouth, and perverse lips put far from thee"* (Proverbs: 4:23-24). We are told to "keep our heart," indicating that we are responsible for it. We cannot blame anyone for how life has turned out. All responsibility for its outcome rests solely on each of us. *"For every man shall bear his own burden"* Galatians 6:5.

Never forget your position as a child of God, bought with the blood and covered with the righteousness of Christ. Know then that you are precious in His sight from the moment of your conception:

Before I formed thee in the belly I knew thee; and before thou camest forth out of the womb I sanctified thee, and I ordained thee a prophet unto the nations (Jeremiah 1:5).

Behold, I have graven thee upon the palms of my hands; thy walls are continually before me (Isaiah 49:16).

But the very hairs of your head are all numbered (Matthew 10:30).

Yes, the battleground is still the mind, and the enemy knows and preys on our weaknesses. When thoughts come to lure us away from the peace of God, let us recognize his intent and motive to turn us away from the mind of Christ. A mind governed by such intent will not choose to conform to the mind of Christ. It seeks to appease the worst part of ourselves without even realizing it. Human thoughts keep us tied to and dominated by the human realm, where the flesh is weak.

Where we are slaves to fear, the torment of death, the works of the flesh, the wicked heart and Satan himself, we open ourselves to attack. The solution is to gain mastery over the human mind with its tendency towards independence and rebellion. This is the state of mind we must seek to attain, when we are in a peaceful place with no background chatter. Your mind is clear and at rest because you have allowed your trust in God to quiet your soul.

A Heart of Love

The heart, according to the Bible, is of the seat of man's emotional and spiritual makeup. It is the place where emotions and desires begin; it is also that which drives the will of man towards action. But more than that, the heart symbolizes the center or core of our being from which prayer and moral actions originate. This even explains the word "core," which is derived from the Latin word *cor*, meaning, "heart."

The human center of being in its unrenewed state is very evil, filled with treachery and deceit. "*The heart is deceitful above all things, and desperately wicked: who can know it?*" says Jeremiah 17:9. In this fallen condition, the heart is beyond human understanding and without remedy. For the fall affected us at the deepest level causing our mind, emotions and desires to be defiled by sin. Many of us are blind to just how severe our condition is.

But, though we may lack understanding of our heart, God does not. He knows the secrets of man's heart. *"Shall not God search this out? for he knoweth the secrets of the heart"* (Psalm 44:21). And through the prophetic word, the secrets of our heart are made manifest ..." (see 1 Corinthians 14:24). God therefore is the only one who truly knows the heart and the only one qualified to judge it.

> *I the LORD search the heart, I try the reins, even to give every man according to his ways, and according to the fruit of his doings* (Jeremiah 17:10).

Jesus knew all men and did not need anyone's testimony because He knew what was in man (see John 2:24-25). He revealed the true condition of our heart in Mark 7:21-23:

> *For from within, out of the heart of men, proceed evil thoughts, adulteries, fornications, murders, Thefts, covetousness, wickedness, deceit, lasciviousness, an evil eye, blasphemy, pride, foolishness: All these evil things come from within, and defile the man* (Mark 7:21-23).

This is what we inherited when our first parents chose to go their own way. We are often oblivious to our condition until the conviction of the Holy Spirit comes upon us and, in that moment, we realize there is none righteous, good or just but God.

To receive salvation, our hearts must be transformed through the power of the Holy Spirit through faith. For it is with our hearts that we believe unto righteousness. *"For with the heart man believeth unto righteousness; and with the mouth confession is made unto salvation"* (Romans 10:10). This deep-seated confession allows God to create a new heart in us in the same way that David after his acts of treachery petitioned Him to create a clean heart and a right spirit within him. We have God's assurance that when we come to Him with a broken and a contrite heart, He will not despise us. In fact, God is more concerned with the condition of our heart than our sacrifices,

> *For thou desirest not sacrifice; else would*
> *I give it: thou delightest not in burnt of-*
> *fering. The sacrifices of God are a bro-*
> *ken spirit: a broken and a contrite heart,*

> *O God, thou wilt not despise* (Psalm 51:16-17).

In the course of creating this new heart He often tests us through humbling processes to see what stuff we are made up of:

> *Thou hast proved mine heart; thou hast visited me in the night; thou hast tried me, and shalt find nothing; I am purposed that my mouth shall not transgress* (Psalm 17:3).

> *And thou shalt remember all the way which the LORD thy God led thee these forty years in the wilderness, to humble thee, and to prove thee, to know what was in thine heart, whether thou wouldest keep his commandments, or no* (Deuteronomy 8:2).

Great emphasis is placed on keeping the heart pure and guarding this wellspring of life. "*Keep thy heart with all diligence; for out of it are the issues of life*" (Proverbs 4:23). Regardless of who we are and what we achieve in life, outside of an encounter with Jesus and the ministry of the Holy Spirit, none of us is exempt from this truth.

God's decisions come from His own heart. He fashioned man according to His own heart, desires, and will. He designed us to live in harmony with His original intent. He also graciously empowered us to have dominion of and to dress and keep the environment He provided for our home.

According to God's intent, the heart is to operate from a place of unconditional love, a love marked by giving, with no conditions, metrics, or merits attached. This kind of love goes against all we have ever learned from the world system for our own self-preservation.

Our primary goal is to keep our heart rich toward God and not consumed with the treasures here on earth that rot and decay.

> *Lay not up for yourselves treasures upon earth, where moth and rust doth corrupt, and where thieves break through and steal: But lay up for yourselves treasures in heaven, where neither moth nor rust*

doth corrupt, and where thieves do not
break through nor steal: For where your
treasure is, there will your heart be also
(Matthew 6:21).

We are also instructed to love the Lord with all
our heart, mind, strength and our soul and to love our
neighbor as we love ourselves as Jesus commanded:

Thou shalt love the Lord thy God with all
thy heart, and with all thy soul, and with
all thy strength, and with all thy mind;
and thy neighbour as thyself (Luke 10:27).

True unconditional love is only possible from a
heart completely yielded to Jesus and governed by the
Holy Spirit. We must be willing to acknowledge the
human mechanics of conditional, calculating love. But
God fashioned the human heart to give and receive
the highest quality of love. Is it possible for it to love
the way He loves? Yes, it's possible once it is changed
and made new. This heart will mirror the selfless and
unconditional love that derives from giving more than
receiving. Thank God we can stand on this great promise from Him!

A new heart also will I give you, and a new spirit will I put within you: and I will take away the stony heart out of your flesh, and I will give you an heart of flesh (Ezekiel 36:26).

God sent Jesus to reveal Himself and His love for us. In giving His life for us, He demonstrated the kind of love we are to give to Him and to others. This love offers a conscious awareness of care and concern for others, giving priority to the well-being of others and not just ourselves. In essence, this love is demonstrated by our deeds. The peak of perfection is its ability to love according to the image and likeness of God.

On His part, God is patient and kind in His dealings with humanity and He does not give us what we deserve.

The Lord is not slack concerning his promise, as some men count slackness; but is longsuffering to us-ward, not willing that any should perish, but that all should come to repentance (2 Peter 3:9).

So what most determines our identity with Him is our love walk. God put in us the ability and desire to walk in total forgiveness until our hearts are only influenced by Him, and not controlled by bitterness, resentment, anger, malice, pride or jealousy. Lord, no man can come to You unless You first draw him. Lord, draw our hearts closer to You. Give us the strength and desire for all that is pleasing to You.

> *Greater love hath no man than this, that a man lay down his life for his friends* (John 15:13).

> *Herein is love, not that we loved God, but that he loved us, and sent his Son to be the propitiation for our sins. Beloved, if God so loved us, we ought also to love one another. No man hath seen God at any time. If we love one another, God dwelleth in us, and his love is perfected in us …* (1 John 4:10-12).

When we dwell in God and He in us, there is no fear in love. If we want to eradicate anxiety, and fear, we need His perfect love. Only this kind of love will cast out fear. When left to itself, fear brings torment.

> *There is no fear in love; but perfect love casteth out fear: because fear hath torment. He that feareth is not made perfect in love. We love him, because he first loved us* (1 John 4:18-19).

Fear is one of the most potent tactics of the enemy against the body of Christ and the world. It leaves open doors in our lives for Satan to enter and wreak havoc in our families, marriages, health, finances, mental and emotional well-being. Always investigate it upon its arrival; never accept it but only reject it and keep it out totally.

Whatever area in your belief system may be without proper knowledge concerning His love, it can be filled with the truth of God's word. It is not something you can earn or achieve but you will need to replace all untruths to overcome fear. Let its strength become your stronghold. You must use the Word of God and replace all falsehood just as Jesus did during the time of temptation by Satan in the wilderness. Fix your mind on Him and only meditate on the validity of who God is and His perfect love toward you. It is only this kind of love that thwarts the assignment by the enemy to promote fear in our lives with the things we encounter.

We must seal this with the fact that all truth is in Jesus, and we have entrusted our lives to His provision, His safe keeping, and His care. The strategy required to defeat fear is His Word. The more we hear it and think on it, the more it becomes a part of us, and the more our faith begins to grow. We have decided to accept the truth of His word and not the lies of the enemy. He made a covenant with Himself to love us. We cannot earn it; we certainly do not deserve it, nor can we accomplish it by any achievement in life outside of our acceptance of Him by His grace. It is simply His love towards us.

This is where we get back to the fundamentals of His incomparable love towards us. I pray in agreement with the writer of Ephesians:

> *That he would grant you, according to*
> *the riches of his glory, to be strengthened*
> *with might by his Spirit in the inner man;*
> *That Christ may dwell in your hearts by*

faith; that ye, being rooted and grounded in love, May be able to comprehend with all saints what is the breadth, and length, and depth, and height; And to know the love of Christ, which passeth knowledge, that ye might be filled with all the fulness of God. Now unto him that is able to do exceeding abundantly above all that we ask or think, according to the power that worketh in us, Unto him be glory in the church by Christ Jesus throughout all ages, world without end. Amen (Ephesians 3:16 21).

Strength and Courage

When the time came for Moses to hand over power to Joshua, he charged Joshua with these words:

Be strong and of a good courage, fear not, nor be afraid of them: for the LORD thy God, he it is that doth go with thee; he will not fail thee, nor forsake thee (Deuteronomy 31:6).

We must take on this same resolve as believers in Christ. Security and faith in God and in His promises is what will fortify us to be strong and courageous in challenging times. Remember, too, the words of Jesus before He departed from the earth,

These things I have spoken unto you, that in me ye might have peace. In the world ye shall have tribulation: but be of good cheer; I have overcome the world (John 16:33).

We recognize we are in a spiritual battle with spiritual enemies with supremely evil intent. We cannot afford to fall apart because we are lacking in an area due to insecurity in God. When we ask for His help, He will fortify us with His love, His strength, and His power to conquer every weakness. We have His promise to never leave us nor forsake us. How can He when we are tattooed in the palm of His hand and forever ingrained in His heart? We need simply to rest in His assurance that He will not fail us, nor will He falter.

We must only believe on the One He has sent. Put all your stakes on Jesus. Take a leap of faith and give Him all of you. Truly He is the best thing that will ever happen in your life. Go all in and get completely lost in Him. Keep your eyes and heart centered on Him who endured everything for the joy of saving you.

> *Looking unto Jesus the author and finisher of our faith; who for the joy that was set before him endured the cross, despising the shame, and is set down at the right hand of the throne of God* (Hebrews 12:2).

Above all, be grateful for the trial you are going through because you know it will pass. But in the process God has begun to work a much more profound and lasting transformation in you.

> *For our light affliction, which is but for a moment, worketh for us a far more exceeding and eternal weight of glory; While we look not at the things which are seen, but at the things which are not seen: for the things which are seen are temporal; but the things which are not seen are eternal* (2 Corinthians 4:17-18).

Yes, Lord, do it all for your Glory!

References

www.biblehub.com

www.biblestudytools.com

www.encylopedia.com

www.explanation.com

www.explanation.com

www.flowingfaith.com

www.flowingfaith.com

www.gotquestions.org

www.harvest.org

www.parableoftheheart.com

www.short-facts.com

www.ucg.org

www.whatchristianswanttoknow.com

Books by Tabitha Henton Lamb

The Surrendered Life

A Pearl of Immense Value

Weathering Life's Storms

Equipping Yourself to Face the Challenges

Understanding God's Plan

Re-evaluating Your Relationship With God

The Purpose of Pain

How God Uses Pain to Strengthen Your Resolve

Enriching the Immortal Soul

A Journey Towards God

Available wherever online books are sold.

Author Contact Information

You may contact the author at:

2008 Airline Drive, Ste. 300 #202

Bossier City, LA 71111

Email: admin@thlministries.org

www.thlministries.org

phone: 318-918-924

Made in the USA
Monee, IL
07 July 2026

56551484R00079